T0160813

Gin & Bleach

poems

Catherine Wing

Sarabande Books

LOUISVILLE, KENTUCKY

Managing Editor
Sarabande Books, Inc.
2234 Dundee Road, Suite 200
Louisville, KY 40205

Library of Congress Cataloging-in-Publication Data

Wing, Catherine, 1972–
  Gin & bleach : poems / Catherine Wing. — 1st ed.
      p. cm.
  Includes bibliographical references and index.
  ISBN 978-1-936747-30-6 (pbk. : acid-free paper)
  I. Title. II. Title: Gin and bleach.
  PS3623.I645G56 2012
  811'.6—dc23

                              2011042165

ISBN-13: 978-1-932511-30-6

Cover photograph by John C. Rieger, 1911. Provided courtesy of the
Photographic Archives, University of Louisville.
Cover and text design by Kirkby Gann Tittle.

Manufactured in Canada.
This book is printed on acid-free paper.

Sarabande Books is a nonprofit literary organization.

The Kentucky Arts Council, the state arts agency,
supports Sarabande Books with state tax dollars and
federal funding from the National Endowment for the
Arts.

for my father & mother,
tonic & root

CONTENTS

Blessed is the man whose hopes exceed his reach,
Blessed is the woman who mixes gin and bleach,
Blessed is the child who feels that he can fly,
Blessed is the steeple on which the sparrows die.

Cody Walker

GIN & BLEACH

Lady Aphrodite,

You who've harnessed the sun and had him as your charioteer, whose tongue weaves a gold brocade embroidered with a syllabub of honey, you who laid your dead Adonis in the lettuce patch and loved him there, who rides the wind on lacewings each knot a spangle, you who yokes a breeze into a settling down and brings a hurricane to blink, Love's summoner summon here some something-out-of-nothing, you conjurer from emptiness and lack, you musterer of a mutual feeling; I'm looking for a bit of overwhelm me, a love-in-a-mist sort of time. If spring can rise from a puddle, from soil in a hard pack, or a scratch of sand then surely you can raise the life from death in me. I'm just a lonely goatherd while the world plays me for harsh. Please lady, even my goats are sly and fail to come when called. For what this farmer in the dell? For what this golden goose? I go round and round the mulberry bush but hardly merry. Come lady, please, to me now, and on this hard care and crazy heart set down a feather tip and quill, soothe a soul's fevered ruffle and bring about some calm sea through which at your bidding a royal fish will swim long and hard to settle by my shore.

Wide Heart

The day rises.
The birds unlace their songs.
The sun conducts the sky
And the heat comes.

The sky hazes.
The clouds sugar with rain.
Everything is silk and honey
And everything hums.

The ocean is full
With the sky. The blue
Is wide and ready
All around us.

Everything rises.
Temperature and pulse
Press against the ground
And grow from nothing.

Summer arches.
The stars flush
As the tide rises
And the moon plumbs

The gathering dusk
Which drops overwhelmed.
The night rises.
Everything succumbs.

Possible Audiences for this Work

The sick, the infirm, the every-day-nearer-to-dead; the delinquent, the depressed, the don't-know-any-better-as-of-yets; the wannabes, the could-have-beens, the have-beens, the never-in-a-million-years; the sickos, wackos, the uh-ohs and nuh-uhs; the deadbeats, the beat-offs, the fuck-ups and shut-ups; the uptights and high-strungs; the strung-outs; the do-gooders gone to seed, the seedy; lagabouts and slugabeds; the stay-aways and shut-aways, the squirrels squirreled away; the hoarders, the pinchers; flip-flops and drib-drabs, the shim-shams; the overdue, the underpaid, the over-and-under whelmed; those who have been had; the if I's, the oh mys, the golly gees; the scorekeepers, the keeper-uppers, the hang-ups and hangers-on; the far-flung, the farfetched; the overdrawn, the awkward and the odd; the *Jesu Cristos*, the Jesus H's, and if I'm lucky, the great god.

I'm

syntax virus after Sylvia Plath

Undertaker, melancholy of mouth,
Ass to the curb, and some-nerved,
Lungs like a hummingbird. A nonsense
Thumbs-up on the don't-don't ode.
A thread unraveled from its bobbin,
Skimming the planet as comets do.
Loud as a pin drop from a prison cell
On No Fool's Night.
Oh low-leaner, broad butter pat.

Clear as day and forgotten like rent.
Closer than a heartbeat.
Upright itinerary, our stay-at-home king.
Loose as a gosling when away.
Like a trap that catches a goose.
A murder of crows, no wings.
Still as an American dream.
Wrong, like naught from naught.
A dirty bird, with my shameface on.

Dominant Tom

Tom's got a new set of rules.
He's put out a fresh lure,

modern gobbler that he is, in hopes
of hooking a big-boss hen. He's shopping

around in a new strut zone. *Make my circuit,*
he says. *Ride my circus.*

There are too many turkeys in his woodlot,
and too much talking trash. A lot of good

the old soft-cluck call will do you. Subordinate
Tom is dead! This new guy is a hoarder

who only takes and eats and eats and takes,
all chest-feather, tar, and lurch. What's at stake?

Your (flatscreen-family-gun-guzzler-SUV) virtue—
if you have one. As Jerry whimpers in the dirt

post-pillaging, he's labeled
soft and easy. Tom just crows and libels.

Trash Bird

Bit of tinsel, twig of hazel,
    Pine cone and a poker chip.
Pleasure center, wrought in shimmer,
    Shine and glister, ketchup drip.

Coffee cup and copper wire,
    Hazard tape and plastic bags.
Egg McMuffin, broken condom,
    Kudzu vine and dirty rags.

Cigarette butt, Butterfinger
    Wrapper and some metal scrap.
Concrete fill and weather stripping,
    Dead mouse in a cheap mousetrap.

Acid rain to acid river,
    Tap water that leaves a rash.
Sewer sludge, smear of vomit,
    Heart of garbage, head of trash.

Under Wrap

Behind an open parasol
an open hand cups and bowls,
in an attempt to behold and solve

for an unknown:
teardrop, globe, or liberty's bell? Regardless,
desire wants doubt overthrown,

and the heart less
(for at least a moment) trying.
Now less one bottom button, the reward's

one breast-pocket full. And as the hook-n-eye
is pinched, the candle shudders in its candelabra.
Nearer and no shying,

the magician's tongue rolls "Abracadabra"
as he—seize her!—vanishes the brassiere.

Fine Point

Let's say
you're the sort
who puts out
too much ink.

The world around
you is awash,
a blotting pad,
for what you think.

Who's at fault:
the blotch who failed
—thin paper—
to absorb your thought,

or the nib,
pointless lackwit,
who bares your doubt
not as a dribble
but a gush?

The Brain Truck

He's all magnet to my brain truck,
polarized and pulled in a stark,
strange-thoughted veer. Lacks ground
and full with impulse. Queer
about the eye, occipital. Never blinks
but ringing. Loads the charge
and smells of sulfur. He needs riddling
and a bottled cork. Requited
to a screw and paperclip, who breed
in his electric coil. Affixed,
riveted, and set. Readyness's ready.
He's neon's key and mercury's
destination. Silver-blooded.
Metal-branded. He bonds me thick.

Petit Zeus

O green o great o grand sea cucumber
called the sky, mouth that opens and closes
upon a solitary cloud, that chews and blows
a whisp into a scud, you who slink at the border
of a day, who spike my night with punch,
maker of a mountain and my dog's flea,
urchin's architect and engineer—ready me,
for far and fathom deep, heap rent and wrench,
place toil, break fear.
                    You twenty-armed, a sun and star,
voracious you, who make a mess like a raccoon,
place me in the lap of tidal lap, o swoon
so sure, your bright-me-out, your leap-me-up-and-far
but I am brittle, broken but a little, and so repeat,
prickle a thorn upon me, your gherkin, sweet.

Conditions of ISH

A bit of blur
or a moment blent
between one minute
and its brother.

Our mingled breath,
sure, doesn't make
making love,
quality of, whatever.

Kind of, is, I think,
not quite. A line
is porous and fickle
with what it wants.

And if wants not,
it must, more like,
approximate and qualify:
a continual re-re-re-write.

These boundaries
are Alsatian borders,
wandering hands,
seeking marching orders.

But moving towards
and towards-er
an ever true and truer
alignment, right?

At least that's
somewhat what
I think I meant
to write.

A Mano

A rock is a rock is a rock.
Except this one's called a hand
and that makes it somehow a part of you,
a member of the band, of which
you're the lead and singer.
It's true it's not too sharp,
more than a bit of a grind,
and it no talk so good. But blunt
though it be, it was made for frankness,
not to prove but to pulverize a point,
to mill and crush any inkling
of an argument into a lovely mash
or sour mush—either way, the matter's bitter.
And how's this any different from
what a tongue does as it hammers out the world,
taking the grain of an idea and gnashing it
against some grammar? Out comes
something about as subtle as a fist,
a dried-out corn-pone grunt,
when the heart called for jam and butter.
Every screw needs a driver, the tongue's
as tired and tied a tool as all the rest.
Language is, at best, a guessing game,
wherein my pen's a rock, a fool, a gist,
trying like a tinsel pickaxe to persist.

Twelve Bar Blues

Today the sun rose old and black.
It had a chicken riding on its back.

Inch by inch he burned up the fog
Then went after a creek, a swamp, and a bog.

He evaporated the harbor, the sound, and the sea.
He took back the glaciers; he was coming for me.

The chicken wore spurs and a tarnished crown.
He dug in his heels and brought the sun down.

I sat on my porch and looked at my hands.
I knew he'd be back to eat up the land.

He mounted the moon when she came in the sky.
She was sent to a room and replaced with an eye.

I've done nothing good. I've done nothing bad.
Was born with nothing, had nothing to add.

The next day was the same but different and worse.
He stole through our souls and our known universe.

Grew small and dim like the light from TV.
I knew that soon he'd be coming for me.

And I've done nothing bad but I've done nothing good.
I was born with nothing. With nothing I stood.

The chicken, he strutted and clucked and pecked
At the world he had saddled, ridden, and wrecked.

We were his egg. He sounded us well.
Then he broke us and ate us right out of the shell.

Vitreous Humor

The eye,
a cup of milk,
a dish of light,

a pool of iris,
flickers, as it writes
its message

to the brain,
express reflection,
refraction's train

of thought. A flash
of focus, a giant
lens for zoom.

Steady pupil
snagged on a plume
of red.

Lucifer's aflame
in a matchstick head
and imagination curls

in a ring of gold,
strikes a vein—
optic nerve

of old—
which twitches,
swerves, and sparks

absorption's
liquid wick.
But the lashes shutter

and lose track
as the closed mind
blinks. Black.

Dance, Misery!

When I made my misery dance she wore
an odd off-white. She was a greedy thing,
not much on the beat. *Hurt this*, my misery
would say, as she swung from hip to hip.
What a wonderment of anguish hung
from her scaffolding. How I wanted
to pluck her and to swallow and how she
sweat like some disaster, lonely in her twist.
And if she teetered on her outward swing
her return was more disheveled. Her lips
were over-painted in a smear of sore
and red. She was lowly on the devil's list.
What has she lost that she keeps calling to?
Her own two eyes, glass, I'm staring through.

Sweet Wish Bean

Even though you furrow
like a snake, and wander
like an ant, even though
you broke the brim of my fedora
when last you drank the devil's
vinegar, even though you thief
through my candle and my light,
I want you at my five-fingered hand.
You are my fork and knife.

You wear me on your body
and strike me with your fear.
You vine me across your wishing-
bone. Let me be a stone
mortared to your chimney.
Let me be new wood growing
into your grain. I've taken you
internally. I've borne your train
of skin and sweat and salt.

And though you cross me
with your black bottle, and though
you weed me from your brass ring,
I am your buckeye and your broom straw.
Switch off the snakeshow. Call off
your rattle. Leave me not
in cheatgrass. I am your silkroot
and your slippery elm.
You are my one-way water.

How Shadow Shot the Aerialist

Who's light without a shadow?
All eye without a blink. Bright.
He'll burn your retinas
straight out of your sight.

He's wingspan without a pair of wings,
more muscle than a man.
His shadow is of shadowy stuff:
dust and dark and sand.

Pull down the shade. Bring up the night.
We're off like a shot flicker,
frantic through the circus tent.
Where he goes is where it went.

A pinball in the rafters:
ping ping plumb plummet.
He's gravity's cramp,
and just as fast he's at the summit.

And catch is caught as close
to near miss as not.
He flies by sleight of hand
though sound of speed and thought.

And we're all suckers—bottom bound—
holding and weighting our breath.
Only his own grave shadow
could run this aerialist aground.

Tom Cat at the Kit Kat Club

It went versa vice at the jazz-o-mat:
neat, up, on the ice. Be Bop begat

Doo Wop and don't be don't be do double-
time. All Apollos and Batwings beat for trouble-

town, of which Tom was king and lord.
Quicksilver was his cabinet man. Nobody was bored.

And even everybody's body odd went rat-a-tat-tat
till the sun came up, down, round and round like an acrobat,

swinging on a string of sound. Sounds like?
A second slipped, a mis-stitch, a tympany strike.

Remember: gravity is light—like a disco ball
and chain. We do it again again till we all fall

down: asses, asses. One more time Tom, hip-hella-cat.
At the megawatt ball he delivers some bad scat.

Self-Medication

When the edge
    is sheered its urge,
what do we lose—
    outward veer? inward nerve?

Does the acute angle
    when cut away
yield an angel?
    And of what use, obtuse?

When the angle's right
    the rig's exposed,
but other-angles-wise
    the verb becomes verbose.

So often what I want
    is to soften
all my barbs and elbows,
    to shave my harp from sharpen,

to sand my corners
    down, and/or
pull my oars in before I sail
    the coarser noun,

which is the opposite
    of smooth, which
shorn makes moot,
    a pointless route.

Is the error
    in the margin?
Are we ringing
    at the fringe?

Or need we whittle down
    the whetstone,
to wit? to what?
    to something we call bone.

Dull is dull, sir,
    in the bowels or at the brink,
and so I'll file my verges,
    with longer vowels but less ink.

To a Wigglehead

after Marianne Moore

You're a polliwog, multi-tasking at the waterlog.
    Frog
        to be, just the tip
            of the tadpole, a brief blip
                between water
                and air. Daughter
            to a triggering tongue lash.
        Song sung of a splash.
    Load
of a head, heart in your ass. Two parts princess, one part toad.

Oh You

Oh scruff, your moth song's sung. You shortcut through my frost to long odds. Your buzz dumb luck locks onto my low moon, but your blood's wrong. You don't. You won't do. But pots of you, my mouth's drunk. Your shout shoots through my lord 'n' jury. My bound-by-thought shuts off, shuts up. You know, don't you? You know you do not do. Your soft knock counts down: my crumb's out, our hour's up. But you cur, you run roughshod up my old song; you don't fuck off you hold on. Thus, knot my hollows. Thus, crown my cup. You bolt my rock. You burn my sun. Your south. My soon. Your should. My ought. But no, no, no, our oughts should not.

Area 25

Hello, seat of my soul,
light of my lights,
instigator of my pulse to pulse.

I'm embedded in your igneous
rock, your solid-as-a-split-pea pre-Cretaceous.
You're the cradle of my me and mine.

Just a little lentil at the summit and crown
of the spine, junction of the head and neck,
this is where I'm told to crow

or sing or not. This pebble is what flexes
my emotional pecs. Shocking. Miraculous.
All these years we've been searching the lexicon

for a soul, putting our bodies on the rack,
only to find it's a slug living
in the drainpipe of the brain. What a fuss

for nothing. All that I have loved
and love has come from you as an electric
shot put, a brief volley

of current and charge. In this election
do I even get a vote? Do you dictate
every square inch from earth to moon to sun?

Am I even now taking dictation?
I know that heretofore my choices
haven't always been good, but wait,

were those yours too? You're no bigger than an ice cube
melting in a bath of whiskey
but couldn't you lift me a bit above the hoi polloi?

Next to you, I'm simple shadow, mere asterisk.
And so I bow to you, little fiefdom of the limbic brain,
Area 25, my neural liege, my synapse king.

My Reptile

Little frilléd lizard
with your big mouth
and your clutch of egg.
Pure urge iguana
—I wanna wanna
wanna—heavy pet
in a moist habitat.
Your dewlap licks
down my spine;
your creep yearns,
yearns your crawl,
like a small machine
that you rev and
rev and rev until
the engine floods.

Still Murmur

Mine own heart's master,
you who bids it beat, and bides
the silence when it beats not,
who circulates the news of news
to my major and minor organs,
who forces breath through my pipes,
who lets it be known when the skin
should flush or the flesh should goose,
you who rouses and floods me, who builds
my pressure up in this the body's
barometer from fair to storm
only later to kill the weather
and his man, you, who,
who boxes a moment up and stores it
in some deep place, who on occasion
makes me tick just like a bomb
but loudly and in public,
who exposes my thin roof and tin
chimney, who suffers me and makes
me suffer—now you drag the chain
and anchor, now release.
You set the wonder-engine
steaming. You stoke these questions
in my chest. You make me ask
and ask who. Who? You.

The Chiefest Word

The most best, winter oyster,
what rings along the nerve.
Deepest seeking, heart-most root.

Zinc and copper. Clawed foot.
What streaks across the synapse,
harnessed to a moment.

Magnetic zero amplified.
Every-any-thing wild, beast
that beats or blurs

or bothers. The newt's
eye, needle in a socket
open wide uninking

on the universe.
A steady bleed. Ever most.
Bestest bet. Cosmos.

Riddle

It comes a long road,
arterial and way. Wanders
deep and surface, but stays
steady. Body. Ready.

Press upon the tide
but the current doesn't
change. The charge
conducts the swell.

In a shell it pools:
fiber, filament, and fist.
Throbbing to your ear,
pacing at your wrist.

Self-Portrait with Doubt

syntax virus after Adam Zagajewski

How does the gentleman feel who stumbles
what sort of song does he sing
does he bugle in whole or half notes
does he go home alone
did he rise from a red tide or
a tide of silence do his limbs still
wear their scars
what country is this gentleman from
is his erudition shallow
does he laugh at his own jokes what does he fear
always this same knife
with the blade's dull insistence does he win
himself over does he sometimes holler in a bitter
foreign tongue how much kindness
does the truth cost him is he in shadow
from what bright light is it on sale
who loves him and for what what's that ink
on his face who snickers behind his back
could you inform him that only cowards
call themselves courageous in public
we all know who he is
see if you can catch him
as he trips and falls in the street

Couplets

If she was his claw and talon,
      he was the polish on her toe's nail.

And if he her post-colonialism,
      then she was post his coronet-colonel.

It was his Jersey shore
      she lay across in her jersey sheet.

And if their lives were jerry-built
      at least the jury was rigged for heat.

Now Now was their common parlance,
      Here Here was their par for the course,

My My was what they called Code Red,
      Aye Aye they called Code Morse.

He wasn't looking for her gas tank.
      She didn't dodge his bullet.

And yet he became her sergeant-major
      And she his gunnerette.

Of course, it's true, they made a mess.
      They soiled every cup.

And when they'd tire of down and dirty,
      they'd clean things standing up.

And so her day his drizzle,
    her fog his afternoon.

He was her oil and vinegar,
    she was his vinegaroon.

Tom & Jerry RomCom

You catch the last corner of her heel as the door
closes. Beat of silence. Then the camera quick-tours

the room: wingback chair, coat rack, credenza.
The stage is set for love and battle. The agenda's

lightning-in-a-bottle and a snuffbox of cocaine.
Enter Jerry, wearing heavy swagger, with a fever in his brain.

Someone has suggested Tom's more than a caper-in-a-
        cupboard
sort of friend. Ridiculous. Don't they know biology's
        boarded up

cross-species romance? Nevermind predator v. prey.
Off limits. Don't work. Cat on mouse. Boy oh boy,

somebody's got some explaining to do, when, *Hello Tom,*
Tom walks out with his Hollywood on.

The world jars. The camera slips into a bedroom lens.
Instamatically Jerry's sold in a single glance—or was it glands?

Love's a match, a whip, a switch-back-blade—out, in—
limited only by how fast-slow a head can spin.

On and Off, Again

Funny, today never stops
coming. One merely adopts

the bearing of the past
until the present's post.

Let's start again. Funny,
yesterday was honey

but today is made of lead.
A balloon becomes a load

of burden, your head a ball
of gas. Nothing at all

to be done about it.
We're in, and then, we're not.

A light switch set to strobe
captures—what?—a microbe

of a moment. And there a kiss
becomes a giant cross

to bear or a flock
of flickers caught half-cocked,

going eternally nowhere.
And that's us, on forever's wire.

First we're on the fritz,
then on fire, then comes the blitz.

There's no moon set
to permanent wax; the sought-

after afterwards sours.
So go the hours.

Counting Song #5

One gun
my life stood and shot through,
Two lenses called my eyes
to see a chain and link,
Three times a day we eat
again again again
Four—ever—or
until ever's over,
Five piggies on your little hand
wee wee weeing
all the way home, a Six-
hundred-square-foot basement,
Seven days a week after
week and never an answer
to the question: what are we here for?
Eight fish to fry and Nine
awkward moments no end
in sight and will we do it
again? Oh yes, Ten.

Night Song

In a clutch of dark the heart grows a bone, the body a knife
for a hand. There's the jabberman alone with his virus,
gumming the fist of the goose-girl, who goes grind
in the night. Ridden and sudden, she's a knot at the end
of a noose. You choose: joint or sinew, dredge versus
bleach, pit or vex. You can't refuse the guillotine, its smooth
discovery, dis-easing you into a world of tremble and surge.
The truth is tourniquet, a trick of the light, and terror is your
    master.
Your company is called Boredom and Disaster. Ask the moon,
that cold vault, if his eye hasn't shriveled from a forever of
    isolation.
The ice-age has only just begun and already fog everywhere.
Never mind. It doesn't matter. What intervenes is not urgent,
just mean. Your ear has grown a cage and in your mouth
that automatic machine gun? That's what's become of your
    tongue.

Death Marching Song

In the old days there were people who specialized in walking the corpse. They normally traveled in the evenings, two guys at a time. One walked in the front, the other in the back, and they pulled the body to walk along, as fast as the wind. They would utter in unison, "Ya, ho, ya, ho."

      —Liao Yiwu, from "The Professional Mourner"

I am a man named so and so,
My horse is called et cetera.
I cut and run. I touch and go.
I gone and went, ya, ho, ya, ho.

Seven dwarves, one white snow,
An apple from your step-ma.
Open casket, glass sideshow.
Fair or not, hi, ho, ya, ho.

I'm the static on the radio.
Listen to my opera:
Do re me, la te woe.
Sing it softly, tra, la, ya, ho.

Once a dodo, today a crow:
Extinction is the formula.
X minus X minus X, ergo,
Negative nothing, ya, ho, ya, ho.

Time takes you in his undertow,
Rows your boat and—halleluiah!
You're ashore aground (in limbo
If you're lucky). Yeah yeah yeah, ho.

The reaper's playing tic tac toe.
The band plays mambo cha-cha.
You dance the danse macabre
To the charnel house cha, cha, cha—no.

Ever onward with the show?
Memento mori and ephemera.
We're at the end times; it's time to go.
Brava! Bravo! Ya, ha, ha, ho.

The Angel at the Air Show

Shows you his underbelly,
Well-riveted oily eiderdown
Down the lubricated length of him.
Stands still before he drops
His everything head first.

The angle's eagle:
Straight arrow earthward.
The godspeed sheers the wind
And breaks through
All your drums and cages.

Blue-point, prick, and needle.
Who asked him to split the sky
And thrill the clouds
With thunder? Who needs the Lord
If he's hench and hitman?

His hornet's of the thrust class
And his only word's a threat. He cracked
The atmosphere. He fractured sound.
We're lost and losing fast. We only
Hear him once he's come to pass.

Eye-Fucked

for CW, the younger

You were just my candy, sweet-tart,
a skittle in the corner of the bar.
I caught you with a dance
and swung you on a star.
You were Mr. Good,
a hard-headed-honey that I bit
while on the beach under a wink
of moon. Soon even the waves
exchanged their tune—a snicker
for a swoon. Is the question
did we swim or did we sink?
Were we suckerfish who struck out
on the sand? (Did we let things
get in and out of hand?)
Or was it just the glint of a passing
disco-eye-ball that cast its spark
and shadow before leading me
down your hall? Help me dove,
my dog-and-pony show's
all laced up in a licorice whip.
Is the flicker of an eye all that love
is made of? A fickle blink of
sweet and spice, just a hint
of lark? Love, I made my eyes for you,
and you, love, you keep
this retina in the dark.

Count Down Song

Ten all rights, better than, Nine no way,
I guess Eight, Seven okay okay,
Six who knows? but Five you know
what I mean, I mean Four,
whatever's Three, and Two for sure,
and yeah yeah, fuck yeah, One.

Moth-Hour

Sing a song of oyster-shell,
    My heart is full of green.
Summon here a luna moth
    With wings of velveteen.

She has four eyes to fly with,
    Two feathers for to see.
She's sailing for a lover
    On a lamp-lit sea.

Sing a song of sifted flour,
    Dust and paper wings.
My head is full of flutter.
    My mind is ripe with spring.

Midnight's in the kitchen,
    Boiling off the fat.
The stars are in my windowpane,
    With Minnaloushe the cat.

Sing a song of meadowlark,
    Pocketful of rain.
The wind is rising in the west,
    The weather's in the vane.

The peacocks and the porcupines
    Are weaving their cocoons,
But I'm waiting for my luna moth
    To fly me to the moon.

Amor, Amar

for S

In your billow my small boat went adrift;
From sure I was alone, afield, afar.
When you left me, I went ajar.

Of me, the soldier was ware.
To me, he was verse. He turned
His circle around my square,

Whiled me sunder, took
Me back and curled in
My ear. My mother settled my look

From akimbo to askance, while the moon
Alighted on my branches in a chorus
Of feathers and wind. Soon

I will make a sea and meet
A sailor to be asea upon.
He will bind me in his winding sheet;

I will abridge him in my arms.
We'll build a shore on which to run
Aground. We'll beach the sun.

Kin is who we're akin to,
A way's a place we make of will,
And it is you astride in me
When I say Adieu.

Cobbled Song

God of the not sun light
God of the not song sound
God of the not moon mystery
God of the not solid ground

Down which back road's shoulder
Should I walk or wander?
At which of the closed doors open?
Which corner have I chosen?

God of the hardening thought
God of the clouding blue
God of the all for naught
God of the all but through

Your Other Other

is the storm cloud's silver lining,
gathering like a crown about your head
(while I hunker down), a clamor
of church bells (when I'm all cow,
clang and clack), is full with (sure)
what I lack, of course (the one I'm off)
is pleasant, gives a scatter shape,
light not like a feather, and
gets the joke eleven times
out of ten, of amore knows a bit,
enough, where and when to have it,
is love's duck and duckling—quack!
(puts me on the counter attack)—
and moreover, she's simply more
(I suppose) than me and better,
shaves seconds off my time delay,
seismically retrofitted and the up-est
to date, she has the latest of the late,
she is, a little like an open vein
of ore, rich, or the best hour of the day.

I guess I'm not the reina
to your ray of sun anymore.
I'm more like the rain on the King's
parade, a Visigoth waiting for the sack,
half a man in a fancy hat, a jewel box
with a stone door, doubtful
diamond, wrecked form. This queen
has lost her anchor and her

anchor stalk. What bird now
will build my wings
and learn me how to walk?

Tom & Jerry Tailspin

Well, it's done. The tongue cannot spin
straw into gold. Your top is not spun

into knowing which way is up. Hence revision:
You're a common toad. And out of fashion.

Jerry can today translates tomorrow
into Jerry can't and never could. Tom rows

his boat ashore and beaches it good. Our characters
are isolated fiascos, the shells of which are about to shatter.

No matter, boys and girls. The story goes (hi-ho)
that we pick ourselves up and start anew, though (hee-haw)

you're still a donkey. Shit. Or a cat and mouse.
Jerry gets around a bit. Tom never leaves the house.

Here, There

Everywhere a special kind of maiming
is going on in a recognizable dark.
It's a monster, but average and bored.
It carries a flail and plays a threshing game.
It cuts us darker till we're spare and part.
Tongue. Torso. It shaves us, wears us, thin.
It hones us to a pin, a single inward point.
It makes a bone spur out of us and out of joint.
Our knot is drawn into a stranglehold.
What we know is pinched and tight. And day
is just a hard stone to whittle a self away on
until it cracks and sinks. You think you're cold?
Touch it. It's in the closet and under the bed
and in the alleyway and in your head.

The Answer to the Riddle

Don't think about the black crow waiting
out on the telephone line. Don't think
about the wig (or how it got there)
out on the lawn. Don't think—
this is important—don't think about
this thing called jubilation or the egg
it crawled from. Don't think
moss or tree-climbing in Japan.
The fling you had with the prize-winner,
also a married man, don't think about
that. Think Dum-Dum instead. Think
haywire. The answer isn't needle
or river or water or snow. Don't think
about the back-alleys you have known.
There is no escape from this honeymoon,
so it's best not to think it. Honeypot
it's not. On the other hand you can think
Can't or Won't. It's not a fog or a shadow
though. The answer isn't fire or Dictionary
of the Dead, if that's what you were thinking.
More along the lines of sparrow in a
chain-link fence, more along the lines of
I'll think about that tomorrow.

The Darker Sooner

Then came the darker sooner,
came the later lower.
We were no longer a sweeter-here-
happily-ever-after. We were after ever.
We were farther and further.
More was the word we used for harder.
Lost was our standard-bearer.
Our gods were fallen faster,
and fallen larger.
The day was duller, duller
was disaster. Our charge was error.
Instead of leader we had louder,
instead of lover, never. And over this river
broke the winter's black weather.

Enough

Listen my pretty pink,
my bell gong, my glass eye,
my much needed rain and sweet
night grass. Here in this space,
this six-inch zone of twilight,
between the sun drop
and moon ball, behind
the no-talent ventriloquist
but ahead of the third-rate thief,
this is what we're given:
penny-ante, mop and broom,
a wooden splinter from which
to carve a self.

I hardly know a way. But
I'm as hot as blood and my house
is clean and waiting. The card trick's over,
the rabbit's gone from his hat but
the next show starts at eight.

Let's plod behind this mule
a while. Let's fall together in a grab bag.
Let's learn a new vocabulary of
asunder and enduring glad.
There's a way, even if such ways are bad.

How It All Fell Out

They opened the emergency exit and sounded the alarm, the escape hatch opened in record time, the window they opened from the top down, they pushed the door open and they left it ajar, they opened the cupboards, they sprung the latches, they let their faucets drip, the chimney flue, the cellar door, these yawned open, they bought the car with keyless entry, they opened the lock boxes and the boxes that were unlocked, they opened their eyes which had been blinking, and their mouths stretched as if to say open, they were outspoken, they let the light pour through, and the air pour through, and that which was neither light nor air they were open to, at the Cabaret Voltaire they were the opening act, they opened vaults and coffins, they opened a funeral parlor and a bank account, a can of Dr Pepper, a bag of chips they opened, they opened card catalogs and dresser drawers, they wore their drawers openly, they opened his will and read it aloud, they opened her attachment and felt that it was strong, they opened a coffee shop when they wanted coffee, a gas station for gas, a bar for a bottle of whiskey, and then they opened the gin, their *Collected John Cheever* was open to the story "The Sorrows of Gin," they were unfastened, unbuttoned, unhinged, undone (his fly was down!), but open most of all, they were open, already their hearts were loose and untied, the moon was no longer called full it was called open, the tide was always high with its own open-mind, and so they unlatched the night from the stars, which no longer shot but went wide.

NOTES

The book's title and epigraph come from Cody Walker's poem "Don't Let Worries Kill You Let the Church Help."

A syntax virus, as I've imagined it, is an exact grammatical replica of a poem not my own, injected with my words. In this case the two source texts are Sylvia Plath's "You're" and Adam Zagajewski's "How Does the Man Look Who's Right."

"A Mano," originally titled "Spoke Saw," was written for the *Manual Labors* exhibit at The Lab at Belmar in Denver, Colorado. A "mano" is a pre-Columbian handstone used to grind corn or wheat.

"The Chiefest Word" is taken from Emily Dickinson's letter (873) to Mrs. J. G. Holland: "I hesitate which word to take, as I can take but few and each must be the chiefest."

ACKNOWLEDGMENTS

Many thanks to the editors and staff of the following magazines that first published these poems:

32 Poems: "The Darker Sooner"
Barn Owl Review: "Possible Audiences for this Work"
Boston Review: "On and Off, Again"
Crazyhorse: "Enough"
DIAGRAM: "Nightsong" and "Still Murmur"
H_NGM_N: "Oh You"
Indiana Review: "Dance, Misery!" and "Tom Cat at the Kit Kat Club"
The Journal: "Area 25" and "Eye-Fucked"
The Kenyon Review Online: "The Brain Truck"
The Lumberyard: "How Shadow Shot the Aerialist" and "Self-Portrait with Doubt"
The Nation: "The Chiefest Word"
The New Republic: "Here, There"
Poetry Northwest: "Self-Medication" and "Vitreous Humor"
Redivider: "My Reptile"
SubTropics: "Counting Song #5"
Swink Magazine Online: "To a Wigglehead"
Whiskey Island: "Riddle" (originally published as "Pulse")

"The Darker Sooner" also appeared in *The Best American Poetry 2010*, edited by Amy Gerstler. "Eye-Fucked" was reprinted in *The Best American Erotic Poems*, edited by David Lehman.

For the gifts of support, space, and time, I'm especially grateful to the Corporation of Yaddo, the Djerassi Resident Artists

Program, the Helen Riaboff Whiteley Center, the MacDowell Colony, the Sewanee Writers' Conference, and Washington State's Artist Trust.

Most of these poems were written for the Seattle Rockshop: Rebecca Hoogs, Julie Larios, and Sierra Nelson. My debt to you is more than I can say. Additional thanks to master precisionist Jason Whitmarsh. Sine qua non—Richard Kenney and Cody Walker.

And finally to Mr. Smith, who is my sailor, my sea, my sun, and my shore.

Catherine Wing's first book of poems, *Enter Invisible*, was published in 2005 and nominated for a *Los Angeles Times* Book Prize. Her poems have appeared in *Poetry, The Nation, The New Republic,* and *The Best American Poetry,* and have been featured on *The Writer's Almanac.* She lives in Cleveland and teaches poetry at Kent State University.

Sarabande Books thanks you for the purchase of this book; we do hope you enjoy it! Founded in 1994 as an independent, nonprofit, literary press, Sarabande publishes poetry, short fiction, and literary nonfiction—genres increasingly neglected by commercial publishers. We are committed to producing beautiful, lasting editions that honor exceptional writing, and to keeping those books in print. If you're interested in further reading, take a moment to browse our website, www.sarabandebooks.org. There you'll find information about other titles; opportunities to contribute to the Sarabande mission; and an abundance of supporting materials including audio, video, a lively blog, and our Sarabande in Education program.